Giovanna Magi

LUXOR

VALLEY OF KINGS - QUEENS - NOBLES - ARTISANS
COLOSSI OF MEMNON - DEIR-EL-BAHARI - MADINET HABU
RAMESSEUM

160 Color illustrations

BONECHI

Photo credits

Photo by Gianni Dagli Orti pages 7; 8; 9; 15 above right and left; 17; 28; 31 above; 32; 34; 35; 36; 37; 38; 39; 43 above; 46; 47; 49; 50; 51; 52; 53; 54; 55; 56; 57; 58; 59; 61; 62; 63; 64; 65 right above and below; 66 below; 67; 81 above; 83; 84; 86; 87; 91.

Photo Olympia Press: page 6 above.

Archives of Casa Editrice Bonechi:
Marco Carpi Ceci pages 14 below; 15 below; 29 below right and left; 31 below; 33; 38; 41; 42; 43 below; 48; 60; 65 left above; 66 above; 68; 69; 71; 74; 75; 76; 77; 78; 79; 80; 81 below; 82; 88; 89; 90; 92; 93; 94.

Paolo Giambone pages 3; 4; 5; 6 below; 10; 11; 12; 13; 14 above; 16; 18; 19; 20; 21; 22; 23; 24; 25; 26; 27; 29; 30; 40; 45; 70; 72; 85.

© Copyright by Casa Editrice Bonechi
Via Cairoli 18b - 50131 Florence - Italy
Tel. +39 055 576841 - Fax +39 055 5000766
E-mail: bonechi@bonechi.it - Internet: www.bonechi.it

Printed in Italy by Centro Stampa Editoriale Bonechi

Translated by Susan Fraser *for* Studio Comunicare, Florence

ISBN 88-7009-617-3

N.B.: in the legends of the Valleys, bold type indicates the tombs described in the text.

INDEX

LUXOR

A strip of green in the middle of the desert, tilled fields and in the background the red rocks of the "Libyan chain". Here lies Luxor, one of the greatest capitals of the ancient world. Charming and evocative, with the Nile banks lined with modern hotels, the feluccas that sail along the quiet waters of the river, the small, silent streets of the Bazaar that come to life in the evening with their colours, sounds and lights.

This is the great, ancient city of Thebes, capital of the Egyptian empire for almost one thousand years, which Homer referred to in the IX canto of the Iliad as "Thebes with one hundred gates" and for which "only the grains of sand in the desert surpassed the abundance of wealth contained therein". The Copts called it Tapé, hence the Greek Thebai, but for Egyptian inhabitants it was Uaset, meaning "the chief town" and Niut, "the City"; it was later on called Diospolis Magna. Its present name of Luxor comes from the Arab El Qousoûr, translation of the Latin "castra" with which the ancient Romans indicated the city where they had installed two encampments.

In the Memphis era it was a small village where the God of War Montu was worshipped and its temples marked the boundaries of the territory. As from the X Dynasty, thanks to its geographical position and political grounds, its importance started to increase considerably until the military successes of its princes made it a great power. Capital of the pharaohs of the New Empire, the god Amon was worshipped in great splendour in the triad in Mut and Khonsu. It was the age of great victories and triumph in Asia Minor, Nubia and Libya. It was a happy period - perhaps the happiest in Egyptian history - and Thebes had no rivals: victorious Pharaohs accumulated incredible wealth there ("city where the houses are rich in treasure") from war booty; from the Red Sea, the Persian Gulf and even from the Sahara - across the road of the oases - merchants arrived to grow rich and to enrich the townsmen of Thebes who reached the incredible figure of half a million!

On the east bank rise the temples in which the gods dwelt whereas on the west bank buildings were constructed for the worship of dead sovereigns; apart from this theory of temples, parallel to the river runs the heavy rock curtain that conceals the Valley of the Kings. Thebes then inexorably fell. The very geographical position that one thousand years beforehand had favoured the birth of its power now became the main reason for its

A felucca, a tourist boat sailing up the Nile and, in the background the rugged mountains of the Valley of the Kings.

Boats heading towards the other bank of the Nile leave from the small landing-stage.

Feluccas on the Nile.

A typical street in the Bazaar. ▶

A horse-drawn cart is one of the best ways of getting ▶
around Luxor.

decline: too far from the "hot" delta region, where the Ramses were forced to create military stations to stem foreign invasions, Thebes lost its political, spiritual and military supremacy. Subsequent dynasties originally came from the delta and the towns of Tanis, Bubast and Sais replaced it as capital of Egypt. Left defenceless, Thebes fell prey to the Assyrian army lead by Assarhaddon, which sacked it in 672 B.C.; once again in 665, Assurbanipal's army deported the townsmen before turning them into slaves and stripped the town of its statues and treasures. Lastly, it was completely razed to the ground in 84 B.C. by Ptolemy Lathyros to the extent that during the Roman era it was a mass of ruins visited by wayfarers; the few remaining townsmen settled in what remained of the temples and the tombs were reduced to stables. This time too, as happened in the case of Memphis, Ezekiel's prophecy that Thebes would be violently shaken came true.

The entrance to the Temple of Luxor, with the courtyard of Nectanebo and the pylon of Ramses II.

◀ *Two pictures of the extraordinary staging of Giuseppe Verdi's "Aida", which the Ente Lirico Arena di Verona brought to Egypt 116 years after its first performance, which took place in the Opera House in Cairo on the 24th December 1871. The opera was commissioned two years beforehand to the Maestro by ambitious Ismail Pashà on the occasion of the opening of the Suez Canal.*

TEMPLE OF AMON-RA

In Luxor, all that remains of its glorious past is the temple that the ancient Egyptians built to the glory of Amon-Ra, king of the gods, and which they called "Southern harem of Amon". Brought back to light in 1883 by Gaston Maspéro, the temple is 260 metres long and its construction was basically commissioned by two Pharaohs, Amon-Ofis III who started it in the XIV century B.C. and Ramses II who completed it adding the porticoed courtyard with its axis moved eastwards, and no longer north-south as in the case of the rest of the temples. The architect was probably Ame-

7

◄ *Detail of the two gigantic statues of Ramses II in front of the pylon.*

The first courtyard of Ramses II with the portico of the templet of Thot-Mosis III.

nophis, son of Hotep. The temple of Luxor was joined to that of Karnak by a long stone-paved dromos, a drome and a processional avenue, flanked by sphinxes with rams heads that the XXX Dynasty replaced with sphynxes with human heads. This street has not been brought to life completely and they are still working on it. The avenue ended at the entrance to the temple of Luxor, marked by the large pylon erected by Ramses II, which features a 65-metre front decorated with bas-reliefs illustrating scenes of the military campaigns of the Pharaoh against the Hittites. In ancient times, the pylon was preceded by two obelisks, two seated colossi and two standing colossi. Today, only the left 25-metre high obelisk is still standing: the other was taken to Paris in 1833 and placed by the engineer Lebas in Place de la Concorde on the 25th October 1836. The two colossi in granite represent the Pharaoh seated on his throne, fifteen and a half metres in height on a base of about one metre. Of the other four statues in pink granite leaning against the pylon, one was to represent Queen Nefertari and another decrepit one to the right, his daughter Merit-Amon. Having passed through the triumphal entrance, one enters the court of Ramses II, with its double row of columns with closed papyrus

The courtyard of Ramses II with the statues of the Pharaoh seated and the statues of Osiris in the intercolumns. Behind the statue of Ramses II, the colonnade of the entrance hall of Amon-Ofis III.

Colonnade of the great courtyard of Ramses II with ▶ statues of Osiris.

A detail of the lotus-shaped fascicled columns. ▶

Before entering the courtyard of Amon-Ofis III, we can ▶ admire this limestone group protraying Ramses II on his own and with the fallen statue of a queen.

capitals and statues of Osiris in the intercolumns. To the north-west of the courtyard one can admire the temple-deposit of the sacred boats built by Thot-Mosis III and dedicated to the triad Amon, Mut and Khonsu. Then follows a colonnade of two rows of bell-shaped columns 52 metres long that take us to the second courtyard, or courtyard of Amon-Ofis II, surrounded on three sides by two rows of columns with closed papyruses, a real, highly evocative forest. From here, across a transversal hypostyle hall, one enters the last sanctuary, the most intimate and sacred part, which gave the temple its name of "Adytum of the south", theatre of the final moment of the festival of Opet, the largest and most solemn held during the year.

The festival, which lasted little more than fifteen days, started on the nineteenth day of the second month of the flood, that is towards the end of August. The highlight of the ceremony came when out of the temple of Karnak came the sacred boat of Amon-Râ which, carried by thirty priests and followed by those of Mut and Khonsu, covered the whole avenue of sphinxes and arrived at the temple of Luxor; here the boats were closed in the sanctuary for a couple of days, before returning to the temple of Karnak, always accompanied by a rejoicing crowd singing and dancing.

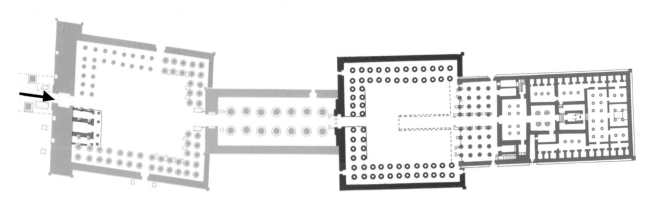

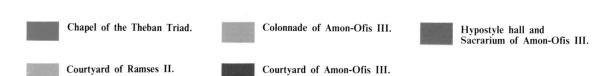

Chapel of the Theban Triad.

Colonnade of Amon-Ofis III.

Hypostyle hall and
Sacrarium of Amon-Ofis III.

Courtyard of Ramses II.

Courtyard of Amon-Ofis III.

◄ The exterior of the temple of Luxor, with its rounded columns featuring open lotus capitals. In the centre, the dome and the minaret of the Mosque of Abu el-Haggag.

In these two photos, the countless fascicled closed-capital columns forming the great courtyard of Amon-Ofis III.

LUXOR MUSEUM

Recently built, this Museum displays countless interesting finds relating to the history of ancient Thebes. The most interesting piece is **Talatat's wall**, a recomposition of an 18-metre wall from the temple of Akhen-Aton in Karnak and destroyed by its successors; the 283 blocks forming it were found in the filling of the ninth pylon of the temple of Amon in Karnak. The wall, formed by hundreds of small scenes, shows work in the fields and craftsmen at work, not to mention Pharaoh and Queen Nefertiti worshipping the Sun.

It is worth mentioning the elegant **head of Hathor** in the form of a cow in gilt wood and from Thutankamun's tomb; a large **sandstone head** with the unmistakeable features **of Akhen-Aton** and a **stone statue of Thot-Mosis I** holding the ankh in his hands.

◄ *The exterior of the Museum.*

The majestic entrance to the temple of Karnak and the avenue of sphinxes.

Detail of the columns in the large hypostyle hall. ▶

TEMPLE OF KARNAK

At about three kilometres from the Temple of Luxor stands the vast monumental area of Karnak, which the Greeks called Hermonthis: the archaeological site includes three divided areas separated by a rough brick boundary. The largest is the central area covering thirty hectares, which Diodorus of Sicily handed down to us as the most ancient one enclosing the dominion of Amon; to the south, still unexplored for about half its extension (almost nine hectares) and connected to the previous one by a drome of cryosphinxes, is the dominion of the goddess Mut, wife of Amon and symbolically portrayed in the form of a vulture; lastly, to the north, the dominion of Montu, God of War, stretches across about two and a half hectares.

In time, the dimensions of each complex changed and the Pharaohs who succeeded to the throne left their mark by extending the temple or adding halls and chapels. The structure of the three holy complexes remains the same: in the centre of each enclosure stands the main temple dedicated to the god and alongside lies the sacred lake for ceremonies usually in a quadrangular shape. Of the three complexes, the one dedicated to Amon is astounding on account of it dimensions.

It is the largest temple with columns in the world and according to distinguished historians, it could contain Notre-Dame Cathedral in Paris in its entirety; Leonard Cottrell affirmed that it was such a vast monument that "it could cover almost half of the Manhattan area"! Not only, but on account of its architectural

16

The avenue of cryocephalous sphinxes
leading to the first pylon.

A detail of the sphinxes with rams' heads.

The sphinxes of Ramses II in the so-called ▶
Ethiopian courtyard.

complexity, it could serve as a base to study the stylistic evolution from the XVIII Dynasty to the end of the Ramses.

A short avenue of cryosphinxes leads to the first and largest pylon 113 metres wide and 15 metres thick, constituting the monumental entrance to the temple; it is unadorned and dates back to the Ptolemy dynasty. The sphinxes with the heads of rams, sacred to Amon, represent the god that protected the Pharaoh protrayed by animals' paws.

The first courtyard that we encounter, known as the **Ethiopian courtyard**, dates back to the IX Dynasty and is closed on the north side by a portico of strong columns with closed papyrus capitals, at the feet of which stand the sphinxes commissioned by Ramses II to flank the entrance to the hypostyle hall. The cour-

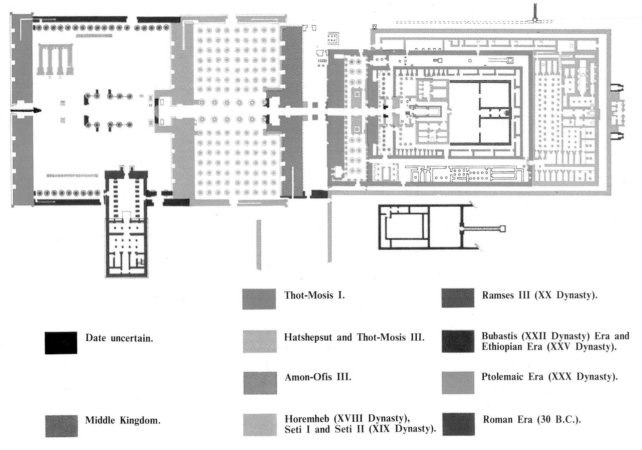

■ Date uncertain.	■ Thot-Mosis I.	■ Ramses III (XX Dynasty).
	■ Hatshepsut and Thot-Mosis III.	■ Bubastis (XXII Dynasty) Era and Ethiopian Era (XXV Dynasty).
	■ Amon-Ofis III.	■ Ptolemaic Era (XXX Dynasty).
■ Middle Kingdom.	■ Horemheb (XVIII Dynasty), Seti I and Seti II (XIX Dynasty).	■ Roman Era (30 B.C.).

The interior of the courtyard and, in the background, the columns of the pavilion of Taharka.

Detail of the columns in the courtyard of the Temple of Ramses III.

◀ *Two statues of Ramses III frame the entrance at the temple dedicated to this Pharaoh.*

◀ *The Osiris pillars supporting the portico in the courtyard of the Temple of Ramses III.*

Following pages:
A detail of the first courtyard, with the huge statue of Pinedjem. The only standing columns of the pavilion of Taharka. A detail of the female statue portrayed between the legs of the Colossus of Pinedjem. The colossus of Pinedjem, High Priest of Amon in Thebes and Pharaoh of the XXI Dynasty.

yard is dominated in the centre by a tall column featuring an open papyrus column; it is the remains of the gigantic **pavilion of the Ethiopian king Taharka**, 21 metres high and with a wooden ceiling destined to protect the sacred boats. In front of the column to the right, one enters the **Temple of Ramses III**, with its courtyard surrounded on three sides by Osiris pillars, where the Pharaoh is portrayed in Jubilee dress.

Leaning against the second pylon, a huge, fallen statue in granite represents Ramses II and another 15-metre high statue portrays King Pinedjem. The 29.5 metre high portal leads to what is considered one of the greatest pieces of ancient Egyptian art: the **hypostyle hall**, one hundred and two metres by fifty-three metres, featuring - eternally challenging time -134 columns 23 metres high. The open papyrus-shaped capitals head, at their tops, a circumpherence of about 15 metres, which could take 50 people standing. It is a real forest of columns, whose dimensions and plays on light and shade create incredible emotions. The central nave, commenced towards 1375 B.C. under Amon-Ofis III who designed it as a simple colonnade towards the sanctuary of Amon, has a different height from the lateral columns which were started under Horemheb, continued by Seti I and Ramses II and finally completed under Ramses IV. This very difference in height allowed the introduction of the "claustra", large open-work windows in sandstone that provide an unreal sort

On these two pages, pictures of the hypostyle hall.

of light. Beyond the hypostyle hall, there used to be the obelisks of Thot-Mosis I, 23 metres high and 143 tons in weight; unfortunately only one of them is still standing. It is surpassed in height by the obelisk of Hatshepsut, which is 30 metres high and weighs 200 tons. In order to build it, the Queen spared no expense, seeing that according to news chronicles at the time, she poured in "as many bushels of gold as sacks of wheat".

Having passed the fifth and seventh pylons (respectively of Thot-Mosis I and Thot-Mosis III), one reaches that unusual environment which is the **Akh-Menu** of Thot-Mosis III, the Festival Hall also called the "temple of millions of years". It is a beautiful hypostyle hall with two rows of ten columns with their shafts painted dark red to imitate wood and a row of thirty-two square pillars decorated with scenes. A few traces of painting of the VI century that have been brought to light on certain pillars tell us that this hall

was transformed into a church by Christians monks.

The **sacred lake** of the dominion of Amon was 120 metres by 77 metres and surrounded by buildings: storehouses, priests' homes and even an aviary for aquatic birds. In these waters, the priests useed to purify themselves every morning before starting their daily holy rituals.

It is amazing that man could have built such a large, imposing building complex; on the other hand, we know that under the XIX Dynasty, 81,322 people worked on the temple of Amon considering priests, guards, workmen and peasants. Moreover the temple benefited from income and a large number of plots, markets and yards, enhanced by all the wealth and booty that the Pharaoh brought back from his military victories.

The architraved pillars of the Akh-Menu of Thot-Mosis III. ▶

The Temple of Amon seen from the sacred lake. ▶

The imposing columns of the hypostyle hall.

In these photos, two statues of Pharaohs lining the Temple of Amon.

The Colossi of Memnon as they appear today, guarding a temple that is something of the past.

THE COLOSSI OF MEMNON

The famous Colossi of Memnon are all that remains of the burial temple of Amon-Ofis III and whose magnificence is recorded in a stele found by the archaeologist Petrie. These statues, which must have stood to the sides of the entrance to the temple, are 20 metres high; their feet alone measure 2 metres in length and 1 metre in width. Cut in monolithic blocks of sandstone and portraying the Pharaoh seated on his throne, with his hands resting on his knees, the south colossus is in better shape than the other, to which a legend is connected. It would appear that in 27 B.C. a terrible earthquake severely damaged almost all monuments in Thebes and that an enormous crack opened up from the top to the middle of the colossus, which it toppled. Others, however, attribute this fact to the barbarities

of King Cambise and this seems more likely as Egypt has never been prone to seismic movements. At the time every morning at daybreak the statue gave out a prolonged sound in which some believed to hear a sad, yet harmonious song. Greek poets soon created a beautiful legend around this strange fact testified by great historians such as Strabo, Pausanias, Tacitus and Philostratus. According to them, the "stone that sings" represent Memnon, the mythical son of Aurora and Tithonus, the king of Egypt and Ethiopia. Sent by his father to help Troy besieged by the Greek army, Memnon achieved great glory by slaying Antilochus, son of Nestor, but in turn he fell under the revengeful hand of Achilles. Aurora in tears then beseeched Jupiter to resuscitate her son at least once a day; in this way, every morning, while Aurora was caressing her son with her rays, he replied to his mother disconsolately by wailing.

In actual fact, the sounds were due to the vibrations produced in the surface which had been broken by the brusque passage of the cold of the night to the heat of the first rays of sun.

The statue of Queen Tiyi, wife of Amon-Ofis III, flanks the legs of the colossus. On the other side, the Pharaoh's mother, Mutemuya.

The decoration of the lower part of the throne: the Nile gods joining in one single kingdom the symbols of Upper and Lower Egypt, the papyrus and the rush.

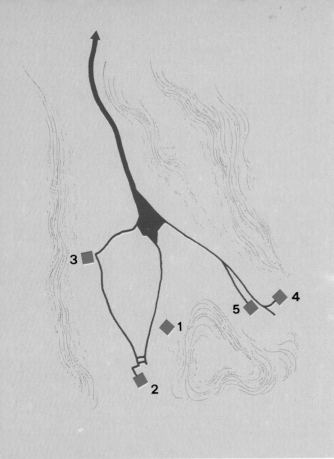

VALLEY OF THE QUEENS

The Valley of the Queens, known today as Biban el-Harim, opens up at about one and a half kilometres south west of the Valley of Kings. The ancient Egyptians gave it the evocative name of Set Neferu, meaning "seat of beauty". From 1903 to 1906 the Italian archaeological expedition led by Ernesto Schiaparelli discovered about eighty tombs, many of which were seriously damaged; some of them featured traces of fire whereas others were reduced to stables. They contained the mortal remains of queens and princes from the XIX to the XX Dynasty; therefore, they can be dated back from 1300 B.C. to 1100 A.D.

Legenda

1 - **Thiti**
2 - **Amon-her-Khopechef**
3 - **Nefertari**
4 - Pra-her-Umenef
5 - **Khamuast**

A corner of the Valley of the Queens and the entrance to the tomb of Amon-her-Khopechef.

Tomb of Queen Thiti

Thiti was the wife of one of the numerous Ramses of the XX Dynasty, maybe Ramses IV. Her tomb, abandoned and reduced to a donkey stable, is well preserved and features an interesting embossed decoration on limestone highlighted by a light pink shade.

In two wall details, the queen is dressed in a light, wide-flowing, transparent dress with feathered head-gear. Here she is portrayed while making offerings to the spirits.

Tomb of Amon-her-Khopechef

Before Amon-her-Khopechef, son of Ramses III, this tomb was built to house the mortal remains of another prince, son of the same Pharaoh. Simply structured - a stairway that leads to a square room and a corridor that leads to the room of the sarcophaghi - the tomb is characterized by a brightly coloured decoration. An unusual sepulchre is the dominant colour in the whole sepulchre.

The frieze on the architrave, with the two cobras ▶ flanking the winged solar disk; in the lower part cobras protect the scrolls with the name of the Pharaoh Ramses III.

The god Khnum with the ram's head alongside Prince ▶ Amon-her-Khopechef: the latter is represented with his hair in a plait, a typical hair-style of young Egyptian boys.

To the left, the Pharaoh, Ramses III, presents his son to the god of death, Ptah.

The Pharaoh in front of Duamutaf: portrayed with a jackal's head, he was one of the sons of Horus and protected the stomach of the dead Pharaoh, contained in a canopic vase.

Ramses III in front of Isis, with a solar disk between his two horns, symbol of the cosmic divinity.

A view of the first two rooms of the tomb. The left-hand pillar is depicted with a large figure of Osiris standing; the wall behind it features Khepri with a beetle's head, personification of the rising sun, and to the right the goddess Hathor of the west with Ra-Harakhti.

Nefertari's tomb

This tomb, discovered in 1904 by the Italian Ernesto Schiaparelli, was excavatd to the west of the valley for Nefertari Mery-en-Mut, the best-loved of Ramses II's numerous wives; it was in her honour that he built the beautiful temple of Abu Simbel. The 27 and a half metre long tomb is to be found eight metres under ground level; it was dug in a very friable layer of rock so that the walls were covered by a thick layer of plaster, on top of which the pictorial decoration takes on the appearance of a relief. When discovered, the sepulchre seemed to have been broken into since ancient times: all the objects had disappeared and the mummy of one of the most famous Egyptian queens had been reduced to a sunder. Only the magnificent paintings bear witness to the fact that this was one of the most important and beautiful tombs in the entire Valley of the Queens.

A corner of the wall portraying, from left to right, the goddess Hathor with Ra-Harakhti, Horus holding Nefertari's hand and Isis. The queen is wearing the royal head-gear that consisted of a feather hat supported by the body of a vulture and a transparent, wide-flowing dress belted at the waist.

Nefertari, in front of a sumptuously-laid table,
offers two globular vases to the gods.

Tomb of Kamuast

Son of Ramses III and probably the younger brother of Amon-her-Khopechef, Prince Kamuast had a tomb similar to that of the kings in its plan, even thought it is greatly reduced in size. Even in this tomb the decoration is very bright, with scenes of offerings and tributes.

Prince Kamuast offers a flabellum to the gods. Like all Egyptian boys, Kamuast had his head shaven and a single knotted plait.

A fine painting of Khnum with the ram's head. The god, guardian of the Nile's waters, is depicted here with a beautiful shade of green, that extends itself to his wide collar.

A corner of the third and last room in ▶ the tomb. To the left Anubis, then Ramses III, wearing the royal nemes on his head, offers two globular vases to Thot with the head of an ibis and lastly, to the far right, another picture of Ramses III with a short wig surrounded by the seshed diadem with the ureus.

Another wall in the burial vault, with ▶ Ramses III and the figure of a young naked boy seated on a cushion in front of which stands a funeral spirit with a lion's head.

MADINET HABU

For many years Madinet Habu was none other than a rich quarry and source of large square stones. During the Christian era, a village, called Djeme by the Copts, rose in this area. It occupied a large part of the site where the temple originally stood and in this way, it enabled numerous vestiges to be salvaged. The monumental complex of Medinet Habut included the **temple of Ramses III**, in front of which stood the **templet of Thot-Mosis I** and the chapels of the deities that worshipped Amon. One is struck with awe by the almost military grandeur of the Southern Gate, known as the Royal Pavilion, which was preceded by a landing-stage on a canal that used to connect it to the Nile. This triumphal gate is set between two towers and crowned by two orders of longitudinal windows. The bas-reliefs sculpted on the walls also repeat the "warlike" nature of this construction, where prisoners were sacrificed, the Pharaoh brought the captured enemy to the god Amon and so forth. The temple of Ramses III, 80 metres beyond the triumphal gate, is one of the most perfect buildings stylistically speaking of ancient Egypt. After a 63 metre wide pylon decorated with war scenes, one enters the first courtyard with the god Thot and the other the Pharaoh with Maat.

General view of the Temple of Madinet Habu.

The 41-metre temple pylons. ▶

Groups of statues of Ramses III with the god Thot.

The second temple pylon, which is also the back wall ▶
of the first courtyard; the 38 rows of hieroglyphic text
narrate the military exploits of Ramses III.

RAMESSEUM

Ramesseum was the name given during the nineteenth century to the funerary temple that Ramses II had built on the west bank of the Nile. His "Castle of a million years" was built by the architect Penre on such a vaste scale, according to Diodorus of Sicily, that it surpassed all other temples at the time. Unfortunately, nowadays very little remains of that splendour: the Osiris pillars still remain on the façade of the hypostyle hall and so does a fallen statue of Ramses II seated on his throne, reminiscent of a defeated giant.

It once measured 17 metres and weighed over one thousand tons. Diodorus of Sicily got the Pharaoh's first name, User-Maat-Ra wrong, and wrote that the statue represented Osymandios.

The first courtyard of the Temple of Ramses III with the Osiris pillars.

VALLEY OF THE KINGS

Beyond the semi-circle of rocks of Deir el-Bahari lies the valley of the Kings, or Biban el-Muluk, which means the Gates of the Kings. This famous gorge, dominated by a peaked mountain called "Theban crown", contains the necropolis of the great Egyptian sovereigns from the XVIII to the XX Dynasties. Its history started with the sudden, unexpected decision of Thot-Mosis I to separate his tomb from the burial temple; moreover, he gave orders to bury his body not in a luxurious monument but in a secret, inaccessible place. His decision rudely interrupted a 1700 year-old tradition! His chief architect, Ineni, dug a well-tomb in a solitary valley, cutting a steep flight of steps into the rock leading to the tomb, along certain lines which were then followed by subsequent Pharaohs. It was Ineni himself who wanted to document the secrecy of his undertaking, ordering the engraving on the burial chapel wall of the phrase "I alone watched over the construction of His Majesty's rock-tomb. No-one saw or heard anything". The latter phrase, however, is hard to believe: it is much more likely that the workers who built it were war prisoners who were then eliminated upon termination of the work.

But, as in the case of the other sovereigns, Thot-Mosis I was destined to reign for a very short time because already in the Pharaoh age, despite the safeguarding of teams of guardians night and day, robbers systematically broke into the tomb to remove the valuable objects: one of the most sought after articles was the "scarab beetle of the heart", the amulet which placed on the heart of the mummy, enabled the dead man to save himself from the day of judgement.

But these powerful sovereigns were destined not even to find peace upon their death. In fact, it so happened that at the time of the weak reign of the Ramses, the priests of Amon had lost all their power and authority. As a sign of their devotion, to ensure their dead sovereigns a quiet life in the next world and to avoid profanation, they started transporting the royal mumies from one burial place to another and these transfers were so frequent that Ramses III was buried thrice!

Finally, they decided to secretly prepare a virtually inaccessible hiding-place: on Mount Deir el-Bahari they dug an approximately twelve-metre deep well connected by a long corridor to a large room. At night by torch-

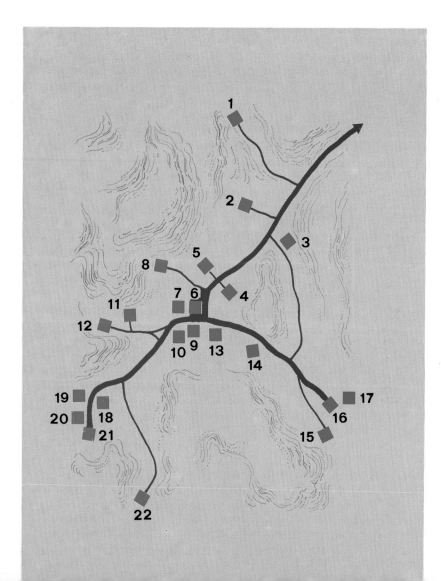

Legenda

1 - Ramses VII
2 - **Ramses IV**
3 - **Ramses III** (never occupied)
4 - **Ramses IX**
5 - Ramses II
6 - **Tutankhamun**
7 - **Ramses VI**
8 - **Mineptah**
9 - Amenmes
10 - **Ramses III**
11 - **Horemheb**
12 - **Amon-Ofis II**
13 - **Ramses I**
14 - **Seti I**
15 - Thot-Mosis IV
16 - Montu-Kopechef
17 - Hatshepsut
18 - Mineptah-Siptah
19 - Sethnakht
20 - Thot-Mosis I
21 - Seti II
22 - **Thot-Mosis III**

*View from above of a part of the Valley of the Kings;
in the centre, the entrance to the tomb of
Tutankhamun that opens up at the bottom of the tomb
of Ramses VI.*

light, as furtive as tomb-robbers, the priests removed the
Pharaohs from their sarcophaghi in the Valley and
assembled their corpses in a cave in the mountains, hanging a shield around their necks bearing their names for
identification purposes. They had been dead for a few
years or numerous centuries and had had short- or long-
lived reigns; some of them had been the most powerful
sovereigns in the entire world. And now here they all were
alongside each other helter-skelter: Ahmoses, the founder
of the XVIII Dynasty next to the conqueror Thot-Mosis
III; the great Ramses II alongside his father Seti I. Al-
together, there were forty Pharaohs' bodies hidden in this
anonymous sepulchre in the heart of the mountain for three
thousand years.

It was a young tomb-robber by the name of Ahmed
Abd el Rasul from the village of Gurnah who came across
that hiding-place in 1875; for six years he and his broth-
ers managed to keep the secret, enriching themselves by
trading the objects that they gradually sacked from the
royal mummies. Then it was gradually brought to light
and on the 5th July 1881, after a long interrogation, the
young Arab led the vice director of Cairo Museum at the
time, Emil Brugsch - brother of the famous Egyptologist
Heinrich - to the entrance to the well.

It is hard to imagine how the scholar felt when the
uncertain light of a torch revealed the mortal remains of
forty sovereigns of the ancient world! A few days later,
the mummies were packed and transported to the valley,
where a ship was to take them to Cairo. And then a
strange, stirring event occurred: on hearing that the
refound Pharaohs were leaving their century-old burial
place, the peasants of the valley with their wives
assembled on the banks of the Nile and, with the slow
passing of the ship, paid homage to their ancient kings,
the men shooting into mid-air and the women wailing
and sprinkling their faces and chests with dust.

Nowadays access is gained to the valley by means of a
comfortable carriage road that largely follows the old
tracks of the funeral procession. The tombs have kept
their ancient charm intact: the countless graffiti on the
walls show that since Greek and Roman times they were
the destination of visitors and pilgrims who left a sou-
venir of their visit in this way. One of them, the English
Dean Stanley, left an account of his journeys in 1856,
affirming that "he had seen the tombs of the kings and
the entire religion of Egypt revealed as it appeared to the
most powerful Egyptian rulers in the most salient
moments of their lives".

Tomb of Ramses IV

It is the first tomb that one comes across on approaching the centre of the Valley. It is small in size (66 metres long) and contains the sarcophagus of Ramses IV, sovereign of the XX Dynasty and son of Ramses III. The plan of the tomb is traced on a papyrus kept in Turin Museum; as from the V century, the tomb was utilized as a chuch by a small Christian community of the Valley. In the magnificent decoration of the tomb, texts are predominant, with scenes from the Book of the Dead, from the Book of Gates and the Book of Caves.

◄ *Seen from the corridor that leads to the room of the sarcophagus: the latter is in granite; 3.30 m long and 2.74 m high (it is the largest in the entire Valley), its lid features a relief of the Pharaoh between Isis and Neftis, the two sisters and daughters of Geb and Nut. On the outside walls of the sarcophagus, figures of demons and scenes of the next world. On the ceiling, numerous scrolls bear the name of the king and on the architraves, the winged solar disk.*

Tomb of Ramses IX

Unfortunately in a bad state of repair, the tomb belongs to one of the last Ramses of the XX Dynasty, whose reign was distinguished by a long series of internal disorders and famine. On discovering the tomb, they found an enormous pair of runners, coming from the skid on which the Pharaoh's coffin was transported and several hundred fragments on which workers working on the king's sepulchre had noted the number of utensils, hours of labour and the list of supplies, etc. The tomb consists of a long flight of steps leading to a corridor connected to two rooms, one of which features four pillars and a second smaller corridor providing access to the sarcophagus room.

The Pharaoh carrying the crown of Upper and Lower Egypt is depicted twice on the corridor vault.

A detail of the gallery wall, with Khnum's solar boat guided by benign serpents and by the ancestors of Hathor and Horus.

The burial chamber with the quarzite ▶ sarcophagus containing the Pharaoh's mummy, the only one still kept in situ in the Valley. The face is covered by a gold mask. The wall frescoes represent the baboons that opened the gates to the next world, the Pharaoh followed by his Kâ embraces Osiris, the wigged sovereign once again with band and short white skirt appearing to the sky god Nut and, lastly, the king's mummy represented as Osiris.

In a schematic, modern representation, the two protector spirits with the serpent Sokaris and the scarab beetle of the rising sun.

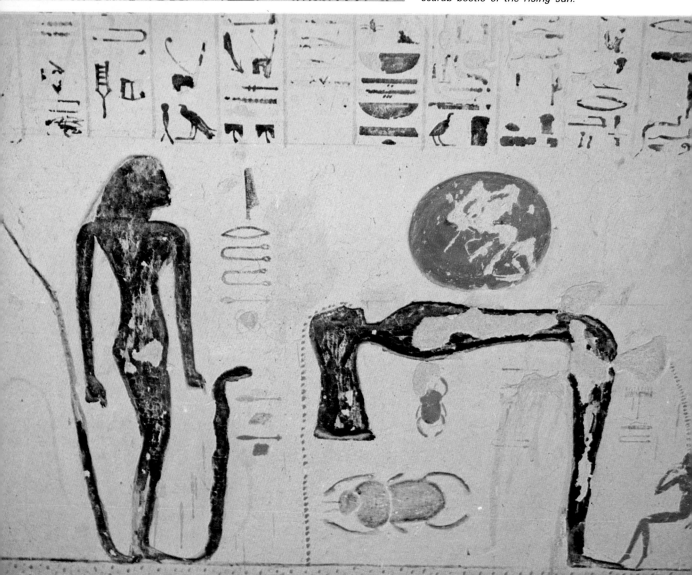

Tomb of Tutankhamun

The discovery of Tutankhamun's tomb was one of the most exciting finds of modern archaeology, enhancd by the enormous wealth of artistic heritage brough to light.

In 1922 Englishman Lord Carnarvon, art colector and great traveller, had already invested about 50,000 pounds sterling in financing numerous excavations in Egypt, all of which had been fruitless. All hope of finding something grandiose, possibly the intact tomb of a Pharaoh, was virtually lost. His missions were directed by another Englishman, the archaeologist Howard Carter. At the time it was common belief that there was nothing left to discover in the Valley of Kings which had been combed high and low. They had still found no trace of the tomb of the heretic Akhen-Aton, who, however, was almost definitely buried at Tell-el-Amarna, and that of Tutankhamun, the Pharaoh of transition who brought back the capital to Thebes reviving the ancient cult of Amon-Ra and the other gods, changing his real name from Tutankhatun to Tutankhamun. His was a short-lived reign lasting only nine years as he died at the age of nineteen in about 1350 B.C.

Lord Carnarvon thus decided that this was to be his last mission in Egypt. The great discovery was made on the 4th November 1922: almost at the base of the tomb of Ramses VI they came across a stone step that led to a second one and so forth, until the sixteenth step stopped in front of a sealed door, walled in with slaked lime. It would appear that this tomb had been robbed, but to what extent? And did they find the mummy intact? On the 26th of the same month Carter had his day: having broken through a second door bearing intact the seals of the child-Pharaoh, the archaeologist made a small opening with an iron bar and pushed it through the hole, meeting no obstacles. He then carried out tests with a candle, not detecting any gases. He finally poked his head through the hole and as his eyes

Another corner of the sarcophagus room, with the Pharaoh between Anubis and Hathor; the latter is transmitting eternal life to him with the ankh ansate cross.

gradually adapted to the darkness, "...strange animals, statues and gold - everywhere the flash of gold, emerged slowly from the darkness...".

"What marvellous things", exclaimed Carter, his voice broken with emotion to Carnarvon who was impatiently asking him what he saw. The marvellous things were the imposing funeral objects which, after long, difficult restoration, Carter sent to Cairo Museum.

Of all the precious objects in the sovereign's tomb, the most impressive of all was the great sarcophagus: a single, enormous block of quarzite housed four gilt wooden containers placed one inside the other like Chinese boxes; only after 84 days of hard toil dismounting them to bring the 80 pieces composing the four catafalques to light was Carter able to admire the

brilliant colours of the paintings decorating the walls of the burial chamber. The sarcophagus was of an extraordinary beauty, "worthy of containing the mortal remains of a sovereign".

On the 12th February 1924, in front of nineteen illustrious guests, a complex winch lifted the ton and a half of granite of the lid. When Carter shone his light on the interior, his first glance must have been most disappointing: only discoloured linen cloths! But when the linen cloths were slowly cast aside, the king and the gold gradually appeared: a wooden sarcophagus entirely plated in gold and inlaid with glass and semi-precious stones with the Pharaoh represented as Osiris, his face expressing great serenity. And yet, affirms Carter, in all that splendour, the most moving thing was a small garland of flowers, possibly laid by his young wife Ankhesanem; after thirty-two centuries, those flowers still conserved a bit of their original colour.

Almost one year later, on the 25th January 1925, Carter tried to open the sarcophagus. The lid of the first anthropoid sarcophagus (2 metres 25 centimetres long) was lifted revealing more linen bands and garlands of flowers. By examining the floral wreaths, they were able to establish the burial season of the sovereign, between mid-March and late April, because botanists also recognised corn-flowers, bittersweets and mandrakes which blossom during that period. Under the sheet they found a second gold-plated, wooden, anthropoid sarcophagus encrusted with cloisonnés of coloured glass and semi-precious stones. With the help of eight men, the lid of this second coffin was lifted; even if at this stage, Carter expected to find a third sarcophagus, he certainly did not expect to find a 22 carat solid gold coffin weighing 1,170 kilograms! "An incredible mass of pure gold": the material itself was priceless! Apart from his head-gear with a cobra and vulture, the king also wears a false beard and a heavy necklace in gold grains and majolica, while holding the whip and sceptre, symbols of the two Egyptian kingdoms; the divinities Nekhbets and Uadjets spread their wings to protect the mummy, while Neftis and Isis are resuscitating the dead Pharaoh. One can just imagine with what awe and suppressed emotion Carter approached the content of this coffin; in fact, he knew that he would have found intact the mummy of Thutankamun. In fact, the mummy was completely covered in gold and jewels. Once again, the delicate, serene features of the nineteen-year old king appeared on the magnificent mask in gold and semiprecious stones that covered the sovereign up to his shoulders. The heavy nemes in blue and gold stripes with the royal symbols on his forehead, inlaid with turquoise lapislazulae and cornelians, made an impressive sight.

Three sarcophaghi, four funeral chapels and kilograms of gold had managed to keep the mortal remains of the great king hidden from the eyes of the world for 132 centuries.

A wall detail with the scene of the first hour of the Book of Amduat: the solar boat with the sun in the form of a scarab beetle enters Amduat, while the baboons open the gates to the next world.

The goddess Nefti opens her arms to protect the eternal sleep of the dead Pharaoh; it is a detail of the quarzite sarcophagus in the burial chamber.

In the sarcophagus room, the left wall is entirely covered by texts on the creation of the solar disk.

Detail of the room with pillars.

Tomb of Ramses VI

Known in ancient times as the tomb of Memnon and also the "tomb of the metempsychosis" by the scholars of the archaeological expedition of the 1798, it was discovered by the Englishman James Burton. On a par with the other great tombs of the Ramses, access was gained to it about 400 metres from the bottom of the valley - exactly the opposite to the deeply dug tombs of the sovereigns of the XVIII Dynasty. The front part is the oldest and was commenced under Ramses V. Having been enlarged, the plan is now quite linear with a corridor that leads to an anteroom, a room with pillars, a second corridor and a second anteroom preceding the sarcophagus room. The latter has an "astronomic" room, that is, entirely decorated with astronomic scenes and frescoes narrating the creation of the sun. The leitmotiv is the sky goddess Nut, repeated twice, covering the eastern and western spheres. The tomb, in which numerous scraps of workers' tools were found, has been visited since the most ancient times, as can be seen from the numerous Greek and Coptic graffiti engraved on the wall.

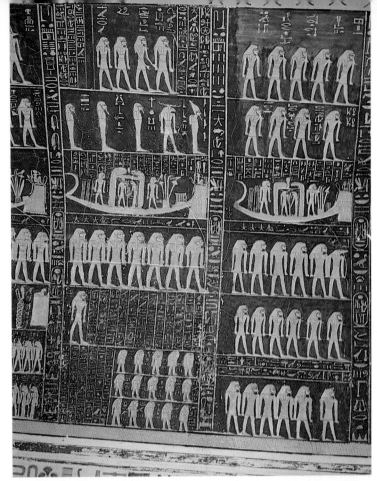

Two details of the ceiling decoration in the sarcophagus room: the two hemispheres with the star gods that form the large procession in the wake of the solar boats.

Tomb of Mineptah

Mineptah, fourth and last Pharaoh of the XIX Dynasty, ruled Egypt from 1235 to 1224 B.C. He was the thirteenth son of Ramses II and Isinofret and came to power at a ripe old age. If his father was considered the Pharaoh of the Jewish slavery in Egypt, his son Mineptah was considered the Pharaoh of the Exodus. In fact, under him the name of Israel appeared for the first time in a granite stele: "Desolated Israel, that has lost its seed". The mummy of Mineptah, which was not found in this tomb but in the tomb of Amon-Ofis II was encrusted with salt upon discovery: this reinforced the belief that he was the very Pharaoh who drowned in the Red Sea while he was chasing the Jews! Apart from the legend, Mineptah was responsible for the military campaign against the "sea nations": the ancient Lybians and their allies, the Lycians, the Achaeans, the Sards and the Etruscans. The tomb plan is simple, a long corridor in sections that descend to the room that still contain the sarcophagus. The scenes illustrated there are the usual funeral myth scenes.

Detail of the room with pillars.

Detail of the corridor that descends down to the burial room.

Tomb of Ramses III

He was the second sovereign of the XX Dynasty and also the last of the great Pharaohs of the Middle Reign. After his reign, there was a confused period of internal struggles and disorders, and Egypt plunged deeper and deeper into chaos. He reigned from 1198 to 1188 and it would appear that he brought about an important administrative and social reform. In the eighth year of his rule, in a fierce battle on the delta, he dealt a heavy defeat to the coalition among the "sea nations" and the Libyan tribes; the battle is recalled in a relief on the temple of Madinet Habu, where some Peleseth prisoners can be seen. Subsequently, they settled in Palestine and were called Philistines. From a papyrus kept in the Egyptian Museum of Turin known as the "Legal Papyrus", we know that during the 32nd year of his reign, Ramses III was the victim of a palace plot: the guilty were captured and sentenced according to the deeds in the papyrus. His tomb is also known as the "tomb of Bruce", from the name of its discoverer, and also as the "tomb of the harpists", from the frescoes

Pharaoh Ramses III portrayed while making an offering.

A detail of the decoration portraying vases and ivory tusks.

that represent - an unusual phenomenon of Egyptian art - some men playing the harp in the honour of certain gods. The Pharaoh's sarcophagus, a magnificent block of pink granite, was taken away from the Paduan archaeologist, Giovanni Battista Belzoni, and sold to the King of France who displayed it at the Louvre. The 125 metre-long tomb drops only ten metres below valley level; this tomb was built on the site of a previous tomb belonging to Sethnakht, father of Ramses III, and one can still see some scrolls in the first corridor.

Picture of a Nubian.

Detail of two Assyrians: the Asians were one of the four human races known at the time by the Egyptians.

Two of the Pharaoh's scrolls.

Tomb of Horemheb

Horemheb, King of Egypt from 1340 to 1314 and the last Pharaoh of the XVIII Dynasty, did not have blue blood. He came from a family of provincial governors and he himself was the head of the archers under Amon-Ofis IV, who was a great friend of his. Once he became a general, he took the place of old Ay, denied the ancient Atonian religion and cancelled the name of his precedessor Tutankhamun, to replace it with his own. One of his most brilliant diplomatic feats was the peace stipulated with the king of the Hittites Mursili II. Right from the moment it was discovered, it was generally believed that the tomb of Horemheb was to be found in the desert near Memphis. It was the English archaeologist Edward Ayrton who found the general's name written in hieratic writing on a tablet relating to inspections of the royal tombs in the Valley. Once it was discovered, the tomb of Horemheb appeared to be the link between the previous tombs and the simpler ones of the XVIII Dynasty and the more important ones which were to follow. In fact, the corridor no longer curves at a right angle, but after a slight initial deviation it proceeds practically in a straight line as far as the sarcophagus room. When discovered, the painted bas-reliefs illustrating the usual scenes of the funeral objects dazzled archaeologists with their perfect, bright, luminous colours, as if they had just been completed.

Queen Isis, mother of Horus and sister-wife of Osiris. Here she is portrayed with the hieroglyphic of her name on her head.

Hathor, whose name Hat-Hor means the dwelling of Horus, is depicted with ox horns and solar disk.

Queen Neftis, wife of his brother Set, bears on her ▶ head the symbol of the castle: her name comes from nebet-het meaning "mistress of the castle".

Pharaoh Horemheb offers two globular vases ▶ to the gods.

Ptah, god of darkness and the highest divinity of ▶ Memphis. He is represented in the form of a mummy, with a cap on his head.

Horus bearing a double crown representing Upper and ▶ Lower Egypt.

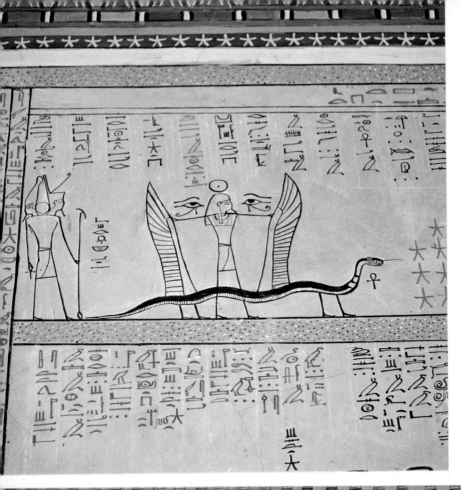

Tomb of Amon-Ofis II

Son of Thot-Mosis III, Amon-Ofis II ruled Egypt from 1450 to 1425. He oppressed a Syrian revolt and made his son and successor Thot-Mosis IV marry Miteniya, daughter of the king of the Mitanni. In the burial chamber is to be found the large quarzite sarcophagus which, when discovered, contained intact the Pharaoh's mummy, his neck surrounded by a garland of flowers. The mummy was displayed in the tomb until 1934, when it was transported to Cairo Museum.

To the left the two-faced Pharaoh, with the double crown of Upper and Lower Egypt, preceded by the solar serpent.

Deities, canopic vases and other symbols of the resurrection.

The sarcophagus room with the wall ▶ decorated with scenes of the Amduat. At the top runs a khekheru frieze, an elegant ornamental pattern in the form of bundles of knotted rushes.

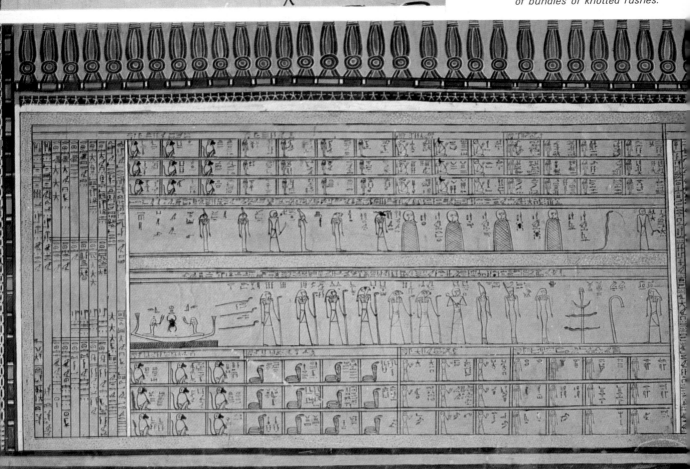

Ramses I between Anubis to the right and
Horus to the left.

A special section from an illustration of the Gates Book.

◄ In the lower part, Atum struggles with the serpent
Apofis; in the upper part, the solar boat with the god
Ra. To the right, the Pharaoh offers two globular vases
to Nefertum, the lotus flower god.

Tomb of Ramses I

The founder of the XIX Dynasty was a military man,
general and vice roy of Horemheb, whom he succeeded in 1314. He only reigned for two years but
during this period - as can be seen in the bas-reliefs in
the hypostyle hall of Karnak - he encroached upon
Hittite territory "as far as the village of Kadesh". He
immediately put his son Seti on the throne and made
Tanis capital of the Empire. His tomb, discovered by
Belzoni, is very basic as the old Pharaoh evidently died
suddenly, while workmen were still busy on it.

One of the pillars of the offerings hall, with the figure of Osiris between two idols of Anubis and seated on the throne.

The figure of Osiris framed in an alcove.

Tomb of Seti I

The tomb of Seti I is the most imposing tomb in the Valley of Kings. The Pharaoh buried there was one of the most important in his Dynasty, the XIX. Son of Ramses I, he was head of the archers and vizier when his father was still alive. He revived the expansion policy in the East, marching into Syria, as far north as Tyre; he drove back Muwatalli, head of the Hittites, and reconquered Phoenicia.

His tomb was discovered in October 1817 by Belzoni: this is why for a long time it was referred to as the "tomb of Belzoni". 105 metres long, a steep flight of steps leads to a much lower level. Here a corridor leads to a second flight of steps that takes one to yet another corridor connected to a hall where Belzoni found a well evidently dug to put people on the wrong track.

The solar boat with the god Khnum with a ram's head: ▶
the serpent surrounds and protects the tabernacle housing the god.

Pharaoh Seti I is portrayed in bas-relief on a pillar ▶
in the first hall.

The boat carrying the dead sun, transformed in Osiris ▶
with a ram's head, sails along the infernal river.

Belzoni noted a 65-metre crack in the other wall. Having adventurously surpassed the well, the archaeologist widened the opening to discover that it provided access to the room that ancient builders wished to keep hidden. However, none of the halls contained the sarcophagus; in fact, Belzoni was only half-way there. New corridors, new flights of steps and other rooms, lastly, led to the sarcophagus which, however, no longer contained the mummy. In fact, seventy years later, the mummy was found in Deir el-Bahari whereas nowadays this outstanding sarcophagus forms part of the Soane collection in London. The extraordinary thing is that this tomb must have been dug even more deeply into the earth. In fact, underneath the sarcophagus ran a mysterious gallery that Belzoni started excavating for about ninety metres, before having to stop due to lack of air and the extreme friability of the rock. A further thirty metres were dug during the nineteen fifties. This gallery has remained a mystery and we still have not found out what purpose it served and where it led. But ancient legend in the Valley has it that the tunnel crosses the entire mountain before it comes out in the open near the temple of Hatshepsut in Deir el-Bahari.

Belzoni maintained that this was the finest tomb to be discovered in Egypt: its decoration, in fact, covered walls, columns and ceilings, with paintings and bas-reliefs rich in meaning and symbolism.

A detail of the representation of the kingdom of Duat and the kingdom of Osiris. The two kingdoms are separated by a wall featuring gates protected by guardians.

◄ *A detail of the infernal gods.*

View of the burial chamber with the sarcophagus.

Tomb of Thot-Mosis III

A steep iron stairway takes us up ten metres above the Valley bottom to the tomb of the Napoleon of ancient times. The illegitimate son of Thot-Mosis II and appointed Pharaoh was very young upon the death of his father; he was ousted by his aunt Hatshepsut, wife of the dead Pharaoh, who confined him to some unknown territory for twenty-two years. Only upon the death of his aunt did Thot-Mosis manage to reconquer the throne; in order to wreak his revenge upon her, he systematically cancelled her name on all monuments, replacing it with his own and that of this father. During his reign which lasted from 1504 to 1450, the country reached the heights of its glory; with seventeen military campaigns in Asia, it was at the very peak of its power. During his eighth expedition, he disembarked in Phoenicia and crossed Syria transporting the ships he had had built in Byblos across the desert. His victories are famous: Kadesh, Megiddo (where he defeated 330 Syrian princes), Karkhemish when he crossed the Euphrates and defeated the Mitanni on their own home ground.

The Egyptian empire also included "the islands of the great circle", that is Crete, Cyprus and the Cyclades Islands. In about 1450, shortly before the end of his reign, Thot-Mosis III ventured as far as the fourth cataract of the Nile bringing the boundaries of Egypt from the Euphrates as far as Napata in Nubia, now known as Gebel Barkal.

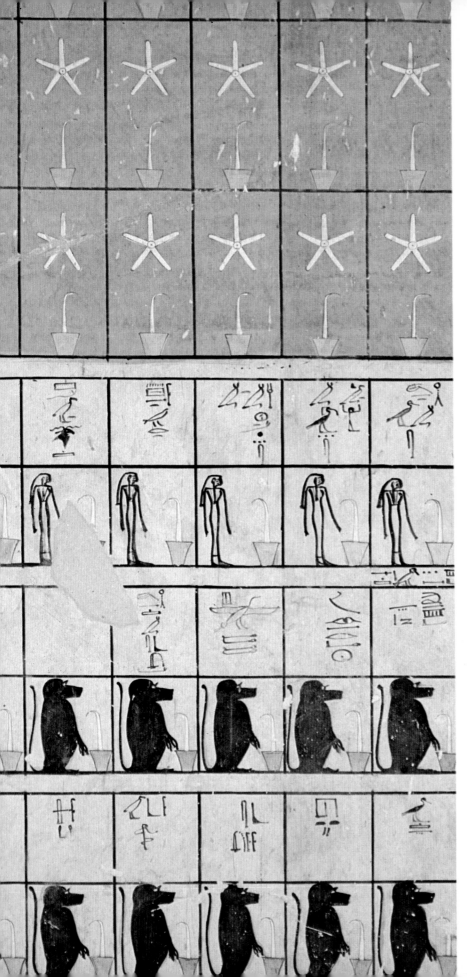

His tomb, dug into a winding ravine at the southern boundary of the valley, features a simple plan; its highlight is the decoration illustrating scenes of the sun's journey in the world of the dead, carried out in a meticulous, almost surrealistic style.

Schematic, symbolic representations of offerings to the cosmic gods (above) and the spirit of the next world and cynocephali (below).

A scene illustrating the fourth hour of ▶ the night: the boat with the sun god with a ram's head descends into the cave of Sokaris.

The serpent Sokaris circumscribes the ▶ "cosmic egg" full of the rising sun Keps-Râ.

A theory of rams with the solar disk ▶ and the crown of Egypt.

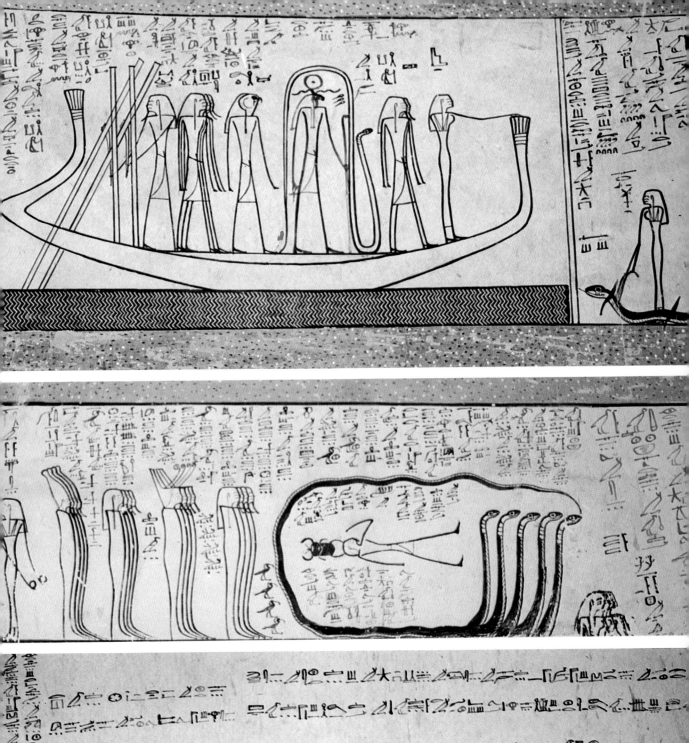

A scenic view of the Temple of Deir el-Bahari.

*Detail of a temple portico, with the protodoric ▶
columns with 16 corners.*

DEIR EL-BAHARI

One thousand two hundred years after Imhotep, another architect, Senmut, went down in Egyptian history with another architectural master-piece. Queen Hatshepsut, more a benefactress of the arts than a military leader, commissioned a monument to be built in honour of her father Thot-Mosis I and for herself chose an inaccessible valley which, consecrated to the goddess Hathor, welcomed the dead in the next world. Having been abandoned, in Queen Hashepsut's monument, they installed a Christian convent known as the "convent of the north", hence the area's present name of Deir el-Bahari; it was thanks to the insertion of the convent in the Pharaoh's temple that it was preserved.

The architect-minister Senmut had the intuition to make the widest possible use of the dramatic range of ochre-coloured rocks spread out inside. The design of the monument was also new and avant-garde to the

extent that the temple of Hatshepsut, called Djeser Djeseru or "the most magnificent of the magnificent" by the ancient Egyptians, is unique in Egyptian architecture.

The temple, which faces eastwards, was a series of vast terraces, which, by means of flights of stairs, ascended to the sanctuary. An avenue of sphinxes and obelisks provided access to the first terrace, enclosed on the far side by a portico consisting of 22 pillars and flanked by two Osiris pillars. On one of the walls, bas-reliefs narrate the birth and childhood of the queen and the expedition that the sovereign promoted in the mysterious country of Punt, perhaps what is known as Somalia nowadays, as they feature giraffes, monkeys, panther skins and ivory objects. On the far wall, 18 large and small niches were supposed to house statues of the queen, both seated and standing. This temple is

characterized by its 16-corner pillars, so admired by Champollion, who called it protodoric.

The entire left part of the valley, however, was occupied by the gigantic burial temple of Montu-Hotep I. Five hundred years before Hatshepsut decided to built his temple in this valley, Pharaoh Montu-Hotep I had the same idea and built his tomb along the typical lines of the Old Empire but tending towards the tombs of the New Empire.

The monumental complex of Montu-Hotep I was formed by a gigantic tomb with a pyramid featuring the king's grave in its centre.

Aerial view of the village of artisans. ▶

The interior of one of the funerary chapels of the Temple of Hatshepsut.

A village along the road to the Valley of the Kings.

VALLEY OF THE NOBLES

In the three neighbouring districts of Assassif, Khokhah and Cheik-Abd-el-Gurnah lie the imposing necropolises of the nobility of the Middle Empire dynasties.

As compared to the Pharaohs' tombs, these tombs are extremely simple from the architectural point of view and all feature the same layout: they are preceded by an open-air terrace, followed by a vestibule whose painted walls describe the earthly functions of the owner. A corridor then leads to an alcove which very often contains the statue of the dead person, sometimes together with his wife or relations. The subjects illustrated in these tombs are characterized by an extraordinary freshness, vitality and realism and provide accurate, valuable evidence of what court life was like in ancient Egypt. The most frequent topics were funeral banquets, with music and dancing, farm work, craftsmanship and daily life in general.

Legenda

1 - **Sennefer**
2 - **Rakh-Mara**
3 - **Usirat**
4 - **Kha-Emhat-Mahu**
5 - **Ramose**
6 - **Neferhabef**
7 - **Nakht**
8 - **Menna**
9 - **Nebamon**
10 - **Kiki**
11 - **Kheruef-Senaa**

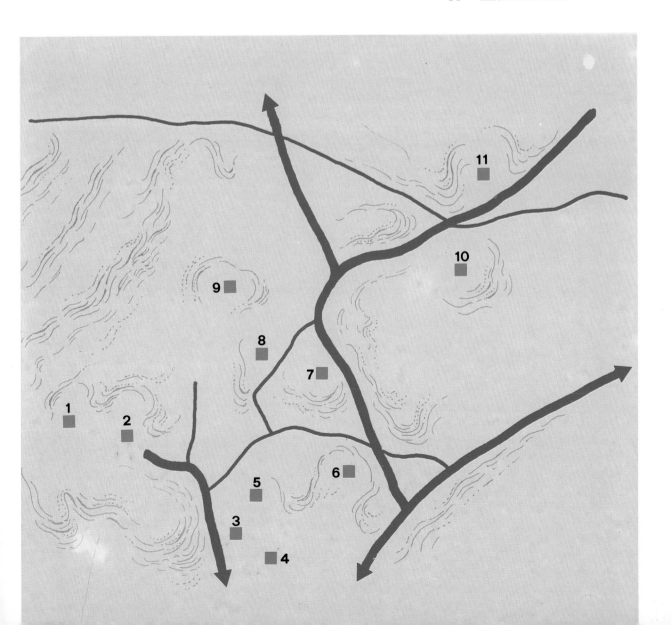

Tomb of Kiki

The tomb of Kiki, the "Royal Administrator", was abandoned for a long time, before being reduced to a stable. It is characterized by lively illustrations in bright colours. An entire wall was destined to illustrate the scenes of the journey of the corpse to Abidos. In fact, the Egyptians were supposed to make at least one pilgrimage in their lifetime to the temple of this holy city, dedicated to the worship of Osiris. In fact, religious Egyptians aspired to having a funeral chapel or at least a commemorative stele in this sanctuary, where Osiris's head is said to be kept.

◄ Scenes of the journey of the corpse of Kiki to Abidos; note to the right the two bearers of offerings and tables.

◄ Detail of the weepers on the boat accompanying the dead to Abidos.

Detail of the ceiling of the tomb, transformed into a delicate pergola of flowers and grapes.

Kiki, portrayed with a short beard, is followed by his wife who is holding a sistrum.

Tomb of Keruef Senaa

Keruef Senaa was the "Administrator of the Great Royal Bride", that is Tiyi, Syrian princess famous for her beauty and dearly beloved wife of Amon-Ofis III and mother of Akhen-Aton, the heretic Pharaoh. The tomb that the Administrator had built is large but remained incomplete; it is worth mentioning the west part of the courtyard, where the celebration of a jubilee (heb-sed) of Amon-Ofis III is commemorated.

A refined bas-relief depicting a conversation among four young women seated on the ground.

Some dancers: it is an interesting detail because it enables us to see the clothes worn by young girls, consisting of a short skirt with plaited braces tied in the front so as to allow the greatest possible freedom of movement.

Tomb of Nakht

Typical tomb dating back to the era of
the XVIII Dynasty, it is one of the best
preserved ones in the entire necropolis.
The owner was a scribe and astrono-
mist of Amon at the time of Thot-
Mosis IV, whereas the wife was a sin-
ger of Amon. At the time of the heresy of
Akhen-Aton, the name of Amon was
systematically removed from all engrav-
ings.
The tomb looks like a classic hypo-
geum and the precise decoration only
occupies the transversal vestibule.

*Picture of a bearer of offerings, holding in
his right hand a bunch of flowers and in
his left a tray of sweets whence a bunch
of grapes hangs.*

*Detail of Nakht hunting among the cane-
brakes in a small papyrus boat. His
daughter is portrayed seated between her
father's legs, while the son on a par with
his father hunts birds with a curved stick
reminiscent of the boomerang: used by the
Egyptians since ancient times and only for
hunting, it looks like a sickle on account of
the two arms bent at the corners.*

Tomb of Rakh-Mara

This tomb, a fine example of Theban civil tombs at the time of the XVIII Dynasty, belonged to Rakh-Mara, Vice roy and Governor of Thebes and Vizier under Amon-Ofis II and Akhen-Aton. Both the vestibule and the chapel are decorated and the paintings are very interesting because they illustrate what must have been the relationships between Egypt and other countries at the time. The most lively scenes depict foreigners bearing offerings: envoys from Punt (Somalians) carrying ebony, ivory and ostrich feathers; messengers from Keft, maybe Crete, with curly hair and long plaits on their chests; negroes from Kush, dressed in panther skin, carrying a jaguar, a giraffe and monkeys and envoys from Ratenu (Syrians and Assyrians) leading two horses, a bear and an elephant.

◄ *A group of workers sculpturing a sphinx and a colossal statue of the Pharaoh.*

◄ *Detail of the garden featuring a basin with water slightly rippling in the wind, and the workers tending to the beautiful fruit trees planted around the basin.*

◄ *Bearers and controllers of funeral objects, which are offered inside baskets and on the tops of tables.*

Tomb of Menna

The owner of this tomb was Menna, Cadastre Scribe under Thot-Mosis IV, who utilized a previous tomb, enlarging it. The scenes depicted are considered some of the most elegant of the entire necropolis on account of their liveliness; they illustrate hunting and agriculture.

A classic picture of a banquet: to the left, a handmaid pours perfumed oil over her master's shoulders. Both husband and wife are wearing on their heads an unusual perfume container, made out of an emptied pumpkin and filled with a perfumed cream that melted in the heat giving off a pleasant fragrance.

The killing and purifying of a bull which will be offered as a sacrifice; the scene is narrated with great naturalism.

Tomb of Sennefer

A flight of 43 steps cut into the rock descends into the tomb of Sennefer, Prince of the Southern Town and Administrator of granaries and the cattle of Amon under Amon-Ofis II. It is also called "tomb of the vine" because the anonymous artist painted a beautiful pergola of black grapes on the ceiling vault.

Under the bunches of grapes, the profile of Seth-Nefer, the "royal wet-nurse" wife of Sennefer and that of their daughter Mutahi.

Husband and wife sailing down the Nile, while a servant presents a sumptously laid table.

Tomb of Ramose

Ramose was Governor of Thebes and Vizier under Amon-Ofis III and then under Akhen-Aton. This magnificently sculpted tomb was never completed; having commenced construction, Ramose had to leave it incomplete to build another one in the new capital of the heretic Pharaoh, Akhet-Aton, now known as Tell-el-Amarna.

A refined bas-relief, implemented before the artistic Amarnian revolution, depicts Ramose seated at table alongside his wife Satamon. Dressed in light, linen tunics, the husband and wife are wearing heavy, ringleted wigs on their heads.

A scene with the servants transporting the furniture, which includes a bed with the characteristic head-rest, four chests and a chair.

Tomb of Neberhabef

The tomb of Neberhabef, First Prophet of the Royal Kâ under Seti I, is decorated in the sumptuous style of the XIX Dynasty.

To the right, the harvest and grape-pressing and to the left the putting into tubs of the harvest and the registration.

In the lower part of the painting, a cart is transported by the bridles; in the upper part the storehouses for storing provisions.

Group of servants paying homage to their master.

Tomb of Usirat

Usirat, Royal Scribe under Amon-Ofis II, had this tomb built; its paintings are extraordinarily well preserved. It features the famous scene of the barber shaving his clients in a garden.

Tomb of Khaemat

Khaemat, known as Mahu, was the Royal Scribe and Granary Inspector of Upper and Lower Egypt under Amon-Ofis III. His tomb, decorated with refined bas-reliefs, is to be found at the bottom of a courtyard onto which other tombs of the same period face. In the alcove of the burial chamber, deeply carved into the rock, one can admire six statues of the dead man and his relations, divided into three groups.

One of the three couples of statues to be found in the niche.

Tomb of Nebamon-Ipuky

This tomb was prepared for two sculptors, both active under Amon-Ofis III and Amon-Ofis IV: the former, Nebamon, was chief Sculptor of the Maestro of the two Egypts whereas Ipuky was Maestro of the two Egypts. Also known as the tomb of the engravers, it is of great interest as its decoration shows us how craftsmen worked in ancient Egypt.

The dead person is purified before being closed in the tomb. In front of the mummy, a woman weeps.

Aerial view of the village of artisans.

VALLEY OF THE ARTISANS

A few kilometres to the south of Cheik-Abd-el-Gurnah lies the valley known nowadays as Deir el-Medina, meaning "city convent" because once upon a time it was inhabited by the Copts of Thebaid. One can see the ruins of the village built at the time of Amon-Ofis I and inhabited by the workers who built and decorated the royal tombs of Thebes. Activities in this valley lasted five centuries, from 1550 to 1000 B.C. and involved stone-cutters, painters and sculptors who reached the necropolis each morning by means of a path that passed over the steep hills around Deir el-Bahari. They left their children and women, who worked in the wheat and barley fields, at home. The workers toiled an eight-hour day for nine consecutive days and the tenth day of rest was assigned to the decoration of their own tombs. The teams of these known as the "servants of Truth Square", were directed by various superintendents and were divided into two groups depending on whether they worked on the right or left walls.

As workmen on the royal tombs, these craftsmen were considered the "holders of secrets" and therefore made to dwell in a village surrounded by walls. Workmen's houses were small and simple; built alongside each other in dried brick, their interiors were white-washed. Generally speaking, they consisted of a tiny entrance, a reception hall, a second room and a kitchen. Sometimes, but not often, they had a canteen and terrace. Nothing has remained of a probable decoration. On the west slope of the valley lies the necropolis. The tombs all consisted of a chapel and a small painted basement.

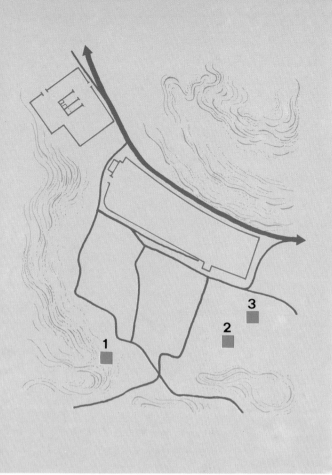

Tomb of Ipuy

A sculptor under Ramses II, Ipuy had his tomb decorated with unusual, curious scenes: even though the style is rather brusque, its wealth of detail make it one of the best-known tombs of the necropolis. One just has to mention the scene of the oculist putting drops in a patient's eyes.

A painting on stucco illustrates a fishing scene with a net. In order to sail in marshy areas, light papyrus boats were used.

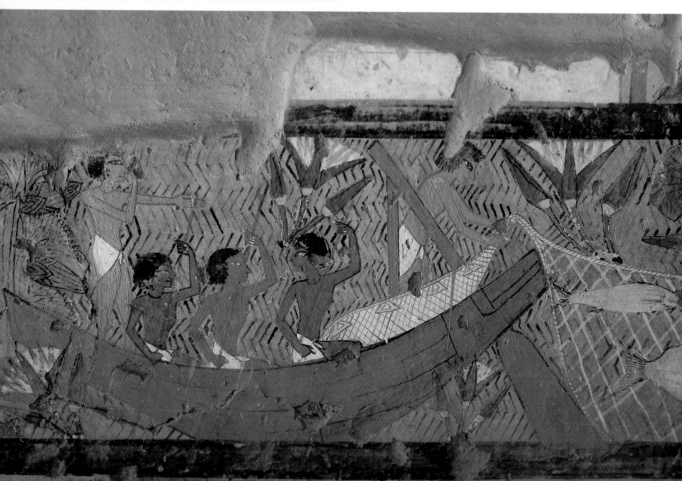

View of the bottom wall of the tomb. Here we can see Sennedjen and his wife in adoration of the gods of the next world. In the lunette above, two Anubises protecting the gates to the next world and two large eyes of the udjat, symbols of the supreme divinity. Of the gods, one can recognise Osiris at the head, whose green skin symbolizes the rebirth of life and, under him, Ra-Horakty.

Tomb of Sennedjen

Sennedjen was a "Servant in Truth Square" and official of the necropolis at the time of the XIX Dynasty; perhaps, on account of the liveliness and freshness of its decoration, it is the most beautiful tomb of the necropolis. The main room of the tomb is more or less intact and is all that remains of the sepulchre; all the furniture contained therein is now on display at Cairo Museum.

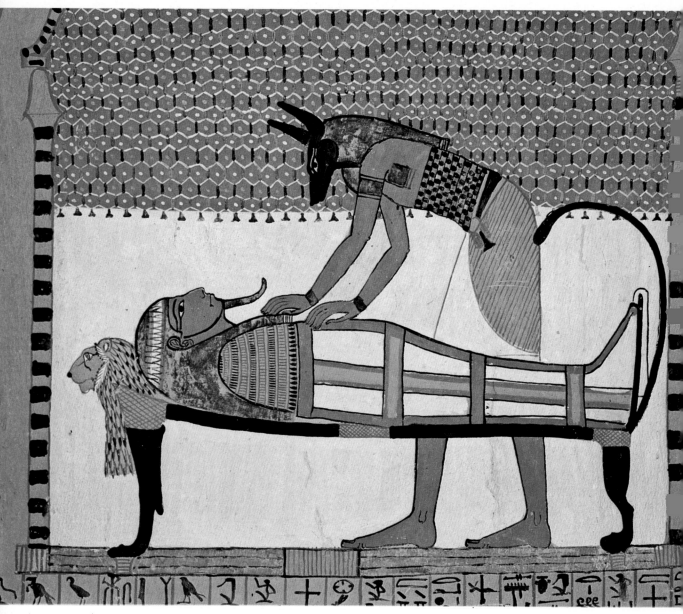

The mummy is stretched out under a canopy on a
magnificent bed with the head and tail of a lion. The god
Anubis, protector of the necropolis, is staring at her and
touching her heart and stomach to wake her up and
accompany her in her journey to the next world. It
describes one of the salient moments of the Egyptian
funeral ritual.

In another detail of the tomb, the picture of Osiris, ▶
portrayed here with his body wrapped in a winding sheet,
his hand and face coloured green to symbolize reborn
vegetation. The god is holding a pastoral crossed with a
whip, symbol of royal power. On his head he is wearing an
atef, or crown formed by intertwined rushes that ends with
the solar disk flanked by two feathers. On both sides of
Osiris, two idols of Anubis represented by two animal hides
hung from a stick.

A priest dressed in panther skin pours perfumed oil over Sennedjen seated next to his wife.

◄ *Two beautiful rural scenes with a deep religious meaning. Sennedjen and his wife working in the fields, ploughing with two white-dappled heifers, sowing and harvesting with the typical Egyptian sickle with a short wooden handle and stone sickle. The wheat fields are lined with date palms, sycamores and the characteristic dum palm. The other scene depicts the growing the so-called "Jalu fields", the Egyptian Elysian fields, the kingdom of Osiris in the next world, to which the dead - once they had been judged and absolved - could gain access and lead a life similar to their earthly lives happily working the fields of Osiris.*

Tomb of Inherka

During the reigns of Ramses III and Ramses IV, Inherka filled the office of "Deputy Master of the two Egypts in Truth Square": that is, he was head of a team entrusted with coordinating the work of workmen placed under him. He had two tombs built at the same time, but only the one furthest downstream and closest to the village is decorated in a lively, imaginative fashion.

A scarab beetle was placed over the heart and was in this way the key to celestial salvation, flanked by Hathor's necklace.

The elegant march of four tall and graceful Anubises.

A detail of the ceiling, with a spiral motif in which one can recognise the head of the sacred bull Apis, supporting the solar disk between its horns.

Two pictures of the solar boat sailing on the ►
blue Nile, in which the dead person is at the helm. In the lower picture, we can see to the right Isis followed by Thot and Khepri with the head of a scarab beetle.

Following page:
In this detail, we can admire to the extreme left Inherka being introduced by Thot to Osiris. The dead man the zed or "backbone of Osiris" hanging from his left arm; it was supposed to bring stability to he who possessed it; Thot, with a head of an ibis and moon crescent, is holding in his left hand a quill and pen case and in his right hand the ankh or ansate cross, symbol of eternal life. Between him and Osiris, a table full of offerings.

A magnificent picture of the martial dance of three Anubises.

MAP OF THE TOMBS IN THE VALLEY OK KINGS

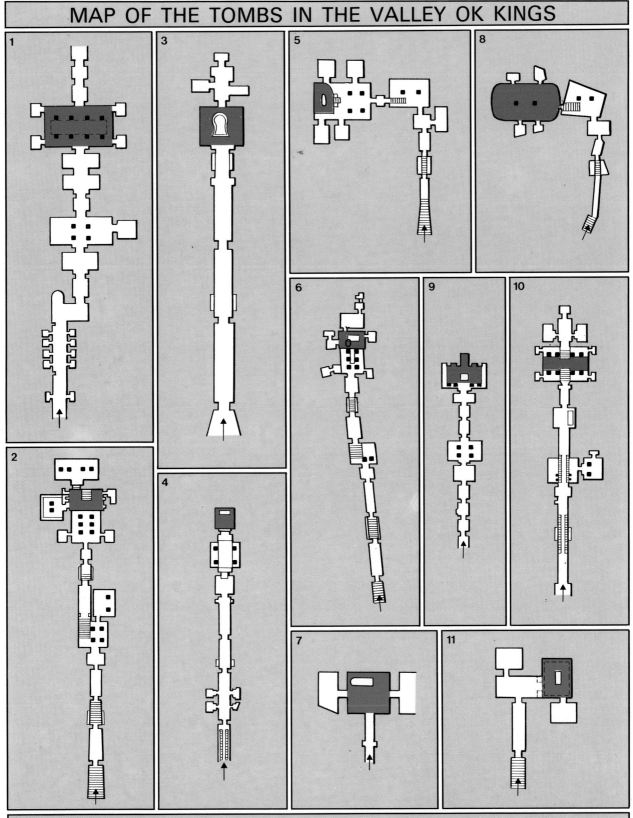

1 - Ramses III; 2 - Seti I; 3 - Ramses IV; 4 - Ramses IX; 5 - Amon-Ofis II; 6 - Horemheb;
7 - Ramses I; 8 - Thot-Mosis III; 9 - Ramses VI; 10 - Mineptah; 11 - Tutankhamun.
The sarcophagus room is shown in red.

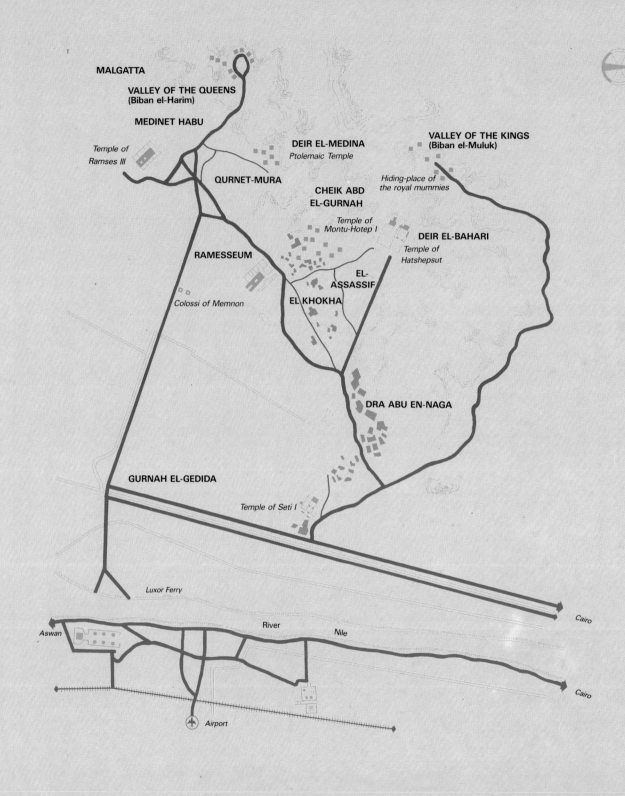

MALGATTA

VALLEY OF THE QUEENS
(Biban el-Harim)

MEDINET HABU

Temple of
Ramses III

QURNET-MURA

DEIR EL-MEDINA
Ptolemaic Temple

VALLEY OF THE KINGS
(Biban el-Muluk)

Hiding-place of
the royal mummies

CHEIK ABD
EL-GURNAH

Temple of
Montu-Hotep I

DEIR EL-BAHARI

Temple of
Hatshepsut

RAMESSEUM

EL-
ASSASSIF

EL KHOKHA

Colossi of Memnon

DRA ABU EN-NAGA

GURNAH EL-GEDIDA

Temple of Seti I

Luxor Ferry

Cairo

River   Nile

Aswan

Cairo

Airport

N